DISCOVER
Yourself

Understand Who You Are, What You Do Well,
and What You Are Passionate About

DISCOVER *Yourself*

SCOTT SCHWEFEL

TATE PUBLISHING
AND ENTERPRISES, LLC

Published by Tate Publishing & Enterprises, LLC
127 E. Trade Center Terrace | Mustang, Oklahoma 73064 USA
1.888.361.9473 | www.tatepublishing.com

Tate Publishing is committed to excellence in the publishing industry. The company reflects the philosophy established by the founders, based on Psalm 68:11,
"The Lord gave the word and great was the company of those who published it."

Book design copyright © 2016 by Tate Publishing, LLC. All rights reserved.
Cover design by Norlan Balazo
Interior design by Gram Telen

Published in the United States of America

ISBN: 978-1-68301-502-4
1. Self-Help / Personal Growth / Success
2. Self-Help / Self-Management / General
16.02.02

Dedication

This book is dedicated to those people who make things happen. Those people who have a new idea, and then take action to make it a reality. It took me 25 years to begin to think and act like them, and then to become one of them–a player instead of a spectator. My first coach in this process was Earle Nightingale, as I listened night after night to *The Strangest Secret*, and then afterwards, because I was looking for more, my wife, Linda. She showed me from our very first meeting in an elevator in Eagan, Minnesota, what life could be like when you have a thought, and immediately move it to action. To those of you who have new thoughts and take new actions, this book is dedicated to all of you: The Players.

Contents

Introduction

This book starts with a promise:

Read it and answer the questions thoughtfully, and you will live a better life.

If you are not living a better life after finishing this book, completing the exercises, and spending 90 days to make it happen, then return your copy *with the completed exercises* to us, and we will refund your purchase price 100%. Find the details at the back of the book.

Have you ever been given a promise like this before? It is the promise of success, if you do the work. By the way, based on statistics only 1% of you will buy this book and actually complete the exercises, even though your success is guaranteed! However, if you are in that elite, committed 1%, (and I believe that you are), then let's get started.

This book is titled *Discover Yourself* and that is really what happens when you read it, and thoughtfully answer the questions. Realize that reading this book alone is not enough, and that you must form new beliefs, new habits and spend the time necessary to learn more about who you are, what you are really good at, and put it all into practice. By following the steps outlined herein, you will begin moving your life and career in the direction of your goals, and attaining greater happiness, job fulfillment, financial rewards and a greater sense of self-worth and personal satisfaction than you ever thought possible. Got a pen? Good, let's go!

You have been asked a very simple question since you were barely able to speak. "Who are you?" is the question, and you have likely answered it a hundred different ways, and your answer has probably changed significantly since you first answered it. The truth for most people is that you probably don't have any idea of who you really are. Think about it. You could answer this question in so many ways, using nouns like father, dancer, sister, etc. You might also begin to think of yourself in adjectives like gifted, curious, or caring. What matters most, is not only the time you spend on reflection, but in seeing yourself through the eyes of others. Self-awareness is a tricky thing, often elusive. In fact, for some people, the more you seek it, the harder it is to find. You may even feel at times like you are running in circles, and then suddenly something happens, and you have a revelation, an insight. Maybe at times like this you sit down and journal, or you share your new insights with others. You might even be prompted to write down some goals in light of new thoughts and feelings you are experiencing. Maybe you have never even written down your goals and aspirations. Not a problem. Using this book, you will begin to discover what your talents are, how to translate your talents into goals, and how to engage a time-tested success formula that dates back thousands of years in order to define and live the life that you are most suited for, and the life you have always wanted, enabling you to give back to the world more than you ever thought you could.

There are eight steps in the process for you to discover yourself. Some of you can get through them in a few days, and for some others it may take weeks, or even months. If you have never really thought about your life as having mission and purpose, it will take you longer. No matter where you are in terms of self-awareness, and whether or not you know your true purpose in life, these eight steps will prove invaluable in your search for a better life and a better you: Let's take a closer look at those 8 steps now.

Step 1. Find Your Passion—What would you do if you had all the money and all the time in the world? What parts of your previous jobs and your current life are consistent with your passion?

Step 2. Define success—in the only terms that matter, yours.

Step 3. Know your personality style, and use this knowledge to better understand why you are here, and what you should do with the rest of your life.

Step 4. Set Goals—Set SMART goals around every area of your life, and write them down. Create personal goals for the following areas of your life:

- Physical

- Spiritual

- Family

- Friends

- Financial/Work

Step 5. Think!—Engage your wonderful, powerful portable super computer brain. Post your goals, and read them daily. Your defined and positive thoughts will begin to shape your daily actions, which in turn, will lead to your successful future.

Step 6. Operate with Integrity—Know that your personal and professional lives are intertwined and that you cannot live these two aspects of your life separately. Choose to operate with character and then, also surround yourself with people and professional endeavors that aim to do the same. Know that every word you speak has an impact on your life and plan to spend your time in ways that have a positive impact on yourself and others.

Step 7. Execute—Lay out a plan that helps move you toward your goals. Remember that your passion and goals will sustain you through the hard times, and understand that failure and quitting are NOT options. Execution is not the hardest part of this program, however, knowing WHAT to execute is actually where most people fail.

Step 8. Give back—Success, when measured by what you alone achieve will never sustain you long term, nor will it enable you to give back. Start now by giving out a smile when you can, a helping hand, and realize you are planting the seeds of giving in your life which will enable you to look back on a long life, and feel it was well lived. We all have something to give, no matter what our present circumstances may be.

Will thoughtfully walking through these eight steps help you *Discover Yourself?* Yes. I say this from my own personal experience, and also because I have heard from thousands of others who have been through this program reporting that it worked for them, too.

I am living proof that the formula works, because I used it to find my wife of 25 years; used it to) raise three wonderful children; to find my way into a career that engages me every single day of my life and to meet friends whom I love and with whom I share the same values and interests. This formula helped me to stay connected to my extended family, live a healthy life and spiritually know that I am part of something much bigger than myself. It wasn't always this way.

Growing up, I never gave much thought to the questions: "Who am I?" or "Why am I here?" I didn't know what I was good at, and I had never made note of any specific life goals. I attended church, but never fully understood my place in things much bigger than the world I lived in. I was drifting through life, often "following the followers," as Earl Nightingale famously said in his epic recording , "*The Strangest Secret*", in 1956. As a result, I drifted into college at the University of Minnesota, and failed miserably. I wrongly studied engineering, having done well in math in high school, but had no real interest in that field of study. I wasn't ready to be on my own, and did not have the discipline to do what needed to be done.

In short, I had no direction, no passion and no plan. Luckily for me, a good friend gave me a cassette tape of "*The Strangest Secret*" when I was 22-years-old, and within 30 days everything in my life started to make sense. I began to live on purpose, with passion and a plan. I graduated, met my wife Linda, started three different companies over the next 20 years, and sold each for more than a million dollars. During the 25 years it took me to grow and staff these businesses, I interviewed literally hundreds of prospective employees, and of the nearly 500 people I interviewed, no more than five understood the principles in this book well enough to make me realize (within minutes) that they were the type of people I would absolutely hire. They were people with purpose, a plan, and the passion to follow it through.

What made me so certain that these interviewees were indispensable? What did they have that the other hundreds who were undoubtedly well-educated and professionally qualified for the job at hand lacked? It was the fact that this small handful of job hopefuls had done their research on my company, and also on all my competitors. They had researched the industry we were part of, (technology, training and consulting), and they knew, without question, that their acquired skills were perfect for the position for which we had advertised. Most importantly, they had done the personal work in advance to **confirm** for themselves that their skills, passions and attitudes were clearly aligned with the position they were seeking, the company that offered the position, and with our specific industry. They were unstoppable; equipped with an attitude that cannot be featured on a resume. These prospective employees were indispensable because they embodied the kind of self-confidence that only comes from someone who is living on purpose, has a plan and is passionate about what they want to do. This is what makes a life worth living, knowing who you are, what you do well, and doing it passionately.

Were you unstoppable, secure and confident, the last time you interviewed for a job? How about when you meet new people, or even in your personal relationships? Complete the exercises in this book, and the next time you interview, or meet someone new, or just spend time with family and friends you will be. You will be living on purpose, and living with passion.

The pre-work that these five successful people did (that undoubtedly secured them a position at my firm) doesn't sound so difficult. So why had all the others (over 99% percent of the hopefuls I interviewed over twenty-five years) failed to do the same?

**Because no one ever told them, or
showed them how to do it.**

I urge you, be that one percent. Understand, acquire, and use the tools you will learn through reading this book to make yourself not only indispensable in the career of your dreams, but to foster an internal peace and fulfillment that only success bred of your personal passion can bring. Know yourself, and live on purpose.

That is why I have written this book, this how-to manual, to share the time-tested formula for achieving your dreams, and to walk you through the same steps which will help you achieve your own life and career goals, and Discover Yourself. The goal is to do something that you love … *the right job*, in the *right* company in the *right* industry based on your unique passions and skills. This formula definitely works, it's been proven millions of times, and you and you alone can determine the outcome, by knowing your unique personality type, have a plan to do whatever you do best, and with passion that will sustain you through the hard times.

Your success will be based upon your commitment to doing the work, and staying the course. They don't call them adages without reason; you reap what you sow, the early bird gets the worm, you make your bed you sleep in it, etc. These are time tested equations for success that will never change. It is just as hard to be looking for work, or working in a dead end job, doing work that you don't enjoy your entire life, as it is to do work that you love, making tons of money, while giving back to your friends and your community. In fact, it is actually *easier* to do the latter, but most of us have simply never had the roadmap laid out for us. It all starts with you.

This book teaches you that there actually is a roadmap to success and self-confidence, and that you are the next person that will again show that anyone can put these principles into place, stay the course, and deliver the results that you want, in a systematic way, and that nothing can stop you from reaching the pinnacle of success for which you are destined. This formula not only works to help you find the perfect career, it also works for you whether your goal is to be a better father, a more loving and caring wife, a successful entrepreneur, or a kindergarten teacher out to change the world.

Please take the time to complete the exercises in this book, even if you are unsure of yourself and your true passion in life. I am convinced that if you stay the course, and complete the exercises you will realize all your dreams, and live the successful life you wish for, using your unique talents to be both a success and to make the world a better place to live.

If you are truly committed, and passionate about reaching your potential, and living a life that matters, please email me with your comments, and more specifically, with the career goals that you develop as a result of using this book, and I will personally support you in any way that I can.

Here's to your success.

Scott

scott@discoveryourself.com

Discover Your Passion

"If you're not passionate from the start, you'll never stick it out." Steve Jobs

If there is one common characteristic among successful people that I have seen in my last twenty years as a businessperson, it is that they have passion for what they do. The definitions of these words however; have become muddy in the modern world. My definition of *passion* is simple. It means *doing something everyday that you love, that you are good at, and that pays you well.* More often than not, "success" is measured in dollars, and the word "passion" is extracted from the formula entirely. I cannot stress how important it is to detach yourself from this assumption (that money = success), because I don't care how shiny your stuff is, or how big your house is–if you don't have passion, you don't have anything. From here on out, when you hear the word "success" I want you to think of it in terms of fulfillment earned through passion, in doing what you love, personal integrity in everything you do, and your ability to give back to make the world a better place.

For most *truly* successful people, whether they are homemakers, CEOs, or athletes, there is a genuine "love of the game" that they all share. What are you passionate about? When was the last time you even thought about your passion?

Two of my passions have always been learning and technology. I enjoy teaching and learning, and I have always sought out the latest and greatest technology gadgets that I could find. It is no surprise that I spent a dozen years, and made my mark in running and owning a technology and training company. The first company I founded, Benchmark Learning, grew to become the largest computer technology training firm in Minnesota. I succeeded in large part because I was doing work I loved.

Do you love the work that you do, or do you, like millions of people, enter your work week with a growing sense of apprehension Sunday night, about 6 p.m., as you wind down from a relaxing weekend, and then suddenly realize that the weekend is almost over, and that you are now confronted with yet another Monday, another day at the office, slaving away for your precious salary. Are you eager to make it to "hump day", and then look ahead yet again to Friday? What a sad declaration about how we as adults relish the "TGIF" mentality. Thank-God-it's-Friday is the saddest statement anyone could make about the occupations we have; the work that we do. The playwright Noel

Coward once said, "Work is more fun than fun." Is this true for you? When was it last true for you? Ever?

When we were children, we thought about our futures with excitement. We were adventurous; we climbed trees solely because they were high and we proudly wore the scrapes on our knees as medals of honor. The term "success" was rarely in our young vocabularies, but in our hearts we knew. We understood that time at the batting cage meant more hits in the game, and that hours mixing the right amount of baking soda and vinegar meant one mean science-fair volcano; we had passion simply because we were having fun. In answer to the question often asked of us by adults, "What do you want to be when you grow up?" We were able to answer in an instant, "Fireman," "Teacher," "Professional baseball player." One of the most successful television commercials of all time was the Monster.com black and white AD that aired during Super Bowl XXXI. Remember the one, featuring young kids, (my daughter, Kenzie was one of them) reflecting on what they wanted to be when they grow up. It struck a chord with literally millions of adults, who had forgotten their long lost dreams of what they all wanted to be when they grew up, and how truly miserable so many of us are in our jobs today. Why is this the case? When did it all go so wrong? Unfortunately, not many of us have the time (or flying capabilities) to wait at our window sill for Peter Pan to come take our hands and remind us of what we once wanted to be. So remember right here, right now (sans fairy dust).

1. Write down what you always wanted to be when you grew up.

   _____

   _____

   _____

   Here's a hint—can't remember? Call your mother, she does.

Note—Since you have already read this far, *only* continue with this program if you are committed to thinking about the questions, *and thoughtfully writing down your answers.* To put it simply, the winners among you will complete the exercises, and reap the rewards. Remember that only 1% of you will complete all these exercises, so decide right now, it's as easy as grabbing a pen, and filling in the blanks. Are you in the 1%, committed to success, or are you bringing up the rear with the other 99%? Change your life, reach your dreams, live with passion, get a pen now and start writing. You are worthy of the 1%, you deserve it.

2. What was it about your childhood dream that captured your imagination? What could you not wait to do after sprinting from the bus stop and setting down your backpack?

    _____

    _____

    _____

3. What unique skills and talents did/do you possess that made you ideally want to do this when you grew up?

_____

_____

_____

Why was it so exciting for you to do?

_____

_____

_____

4. What do you do today, or what was the last job you had?

_____

_____

_____

5. What aspects of what you do now (or did) if any, are similar to your childhood dream?

    _____

    _____

    _____

6. Are you in the right job today, or was the last job you had just right for you.

    Yes, or No? Why, what was missing?

    _____

    _____

    _____

I am not suggesting that we all hate our jobs, but how many of us truly *love* the work that we do. Do you? Did you? Would you do that job if you weren't paid to show up for work? I used to have a plaque on my office wall that said, "TGIM", or Thank God it's Monday! How many of us would hang the same plaque up, and believe it? Would any of us even show up to work if we didn't get paid?

It's troubling that millions of people reserve their hearts and their spirits for weekend pursuits, or for their after work commitments, like scouting or sports. They save up energy all week long, to be released in precious small doses wrapped around a hobby for which the passion still applies. When did we forget that our passions can and should include what we do as work or as a career?

Here's an easy question to help you make this relevant. If you won $500,000,000 in the lottery, would you keep the same job that you are in now? Would you? Some people, less than 1% of those asked this question, can say, "Yes." It doesn't matter what job you have, what matters is you would do it if you never *had* to work again a day in your life. That is the job we are now looking for. It's the job you are so good at that you do it nights and weekends, with little or no effort. It's the job that causes you to lose track of yourself, and even lose track of time. It's the perfect job for you, and believe me, it is really out there.

Here's a case in point: I asked someone years ago, "What do you *really* want to be doing with your life?" At the time the person was selling computer software, and doing fairly well at it.

He answered, "Well, when I have $500,000 in the bank I'll be a history teacher for students in 7th and 8th grade."

I then asked, "Why don't you do that right now?"

"I really love teaching, and I love history, but I just can't stand the idea of living now on a teacher's salary," he responded.

Seems like a dead end for his dream, doesn't it? Not at all. I suggested that he print up flyers, announcing a trip for 7th and 8th graders to Washington, D.C. to study history for one week in a group that he would lead, and distribute them in well-to-do neighborhoods, or run a small AD in a local magazine or newspaper. We did some very quick math and he soon realized that if he could get just 10-12 students at $1500 each that he could earn more than he was making in his current job, and take three months off every year! Did he do it? No. Why not? Because he was not *sure* that it was what he should be doing. He was not clear on who he is, what his true talents are, and what he is really passionate about. We'll never know if it would have worked or not, but it illustrates that anything is possible if you look at it from a new perspective. What thoughts are holding you back? What would you do if you knew that you couldn't fail?

Another example that comes to mind is another friend whose nine-year-old daughter came home from school very sad. When her mom asked why, she said it was because she wanted to be a poet, but the other kids at school told her that poets never make any money. She was devastated. Her mom asked her if they could see if this idea, "that poets never make any money" was actually true. She had her daughter write a few poems, and together they went to their local copy shop and made a few boxes of stationery, featuring her daughter's poems. Then they went door to door in her neighborhood, and sold all of them! After the costs of the printing, her daughter made almost $20 dollars! The lesson stuck, and at age 12, just three years later, this little girl sold over $90,000 of cards and stationery!

What limiting beliefs are holding you back from pursuing your dream job? The one I hear most often is, "I can't start something new because I am so busy doing my day job," or, "I can't quit what I do now to do whatever it is that I would really love to do." These are all limiting beliefs, and all easy to overcome with possibility thinking.

Just this week I was flying next to a woman who was on her way to meet with her corporate office after selling their products for 24 years. She was unhappy with the new way she was being managed, and wanted to find a new way forward. She explained to me, "This is a huge problem for me right now, and I wish it wasn't happening?" We talked for an hour about what she was really passionate about, and what she did well, and eventually she realized that this meeting she was going to have was not actually a huge problem, but actually the perfect opportunity to begin living the life of her dreams, working independently, contracting herself back to clients and spending much more time with her young daughter. Knowing herself, her skills and her passion guided her what to do next.

When Fred Smith told people that he was going to deliver packages all across the United States people told him he was crazy. He did it anyway, and FedEx was born. He followed his passion, his dream, and it worked. Sometimes you have to be a little crazy to get what you want. If you are always blending in, it means you are in the 99% of people, and not in the 1%, but I believe that you are in that 1%. Doing something that others say sounds crazy may lead to you living the life of your dreams.

Write down ten things about which you are passionate right now, not ten jobs, but ten "anythings". Thinking of them puts a smile on your face, and your heart beats a little faster. You wish you could go and do more of these things, and they may even be your hobbies or a sport that you love. People, places, things, activities—it doesn't matter, it's just what you are passionate about right now:

1. _____

2. _____

3. _____

4. _____

5. _____

6. _____

7. _____

8. _____

9. _____

10._____

7. If you could have any job in the world right now, what would it be? Be very specific, what job in what place, and exactly what would you be doing every day?

_____

_____

_____

8. Why?

_____

_____

_____

A friend of mine, teaches a seminar on creativity that he begins with a description of babies. He says, "Babies scream a lot, they poop in their pants, spit up, and yet, when someone introduces their new baby to friends, we all say, 'Isn't she a miracle?' and, 'What a beautiful, wonderful baby?'"

My friend then asks the question in his seminar, "When did we stop being miracles? When did we lose our dreams, and our passion? When, and more importantly, *why* did we cease to be miracles?"

Try right now to think of yourself as a miracle of creation. It is impossible for most of us to fathom, but there was a time when it was true for you, and I believe it still is. I believe that you are not here by chance. None of us are. Of all the billions of people on this earth, literally billions, you are unique. You possess unique gifts and talents that are yours and yours alone, and you can change your future by your will alone. Don't believe it? If you are sitting down right now, stand up! STAND UP, or at least LOOK UP! Do it now! 1% will, but 99% will not. What started out as a new thought, *I think I'll stand up* …just happened. It started as your unique thought, and then it happened. Out of the billions of people in the world, you are free to have a new thought, your very own thought, and then make it happen. Wow. Infinite possibilities, always.

As you consider your unique talents, and the position in life that would ideally suit you best, consider a quote on the next page from Marianne Williamson's, *A Return to Love:*

Our deepest fear is not that we are inadequate.
Our deepest fear
is that we are powerful beyond measure.
It is our light, not our darkness,
that most frightens us.
We ask ourselves, who am I
to be brilliant, gorgeous,
talented and fabulous?
Actually, who are you not to be?
You are a child of God.
Your playing small doesn't serve the world.
There is nothing enlightened about shrinking
so that other people won't feel insecure around
you. You are meant to shine, as children do.
We were born to make manifest
the glory of God that is within us.

It's not just in some of us; it's in everyone.
And as we let our own light shine,
we unconsciously give other people
permission to do the same.
As we are liberated from our own fear,
our presence automatically liberates others.

9. Think long and hard about what unique gifts and talents you bring to the world. Ask yourself, your spouse and your friends and family what they feel you do best, and then evaluate yourself on what you do, and what you do not do well, and then write down your honest results here. Assessing yourself in this way may bring about some anxiety, but don't pout! The most precious and valuable gift you can give yourself is the power to realize your true potential, and the tools necessary to create wonders with it. Try and define both your strengths and weaknesses simply, such as, *enjoys meeting new people, works well alone, likes details, loves the outdoors, can't remember details, good at math, creative, hardworking,*

procrastinates, etc. Go with your first impressions, and try not to over think the basic likes and dislikes, and talents and skills gaps you have:

Your Strengths   Your Potential
                                  Weaknesses

_____   _____

_____   _____

_____   _____

_____   _____

_____   _____

_____   _____

_____   _____

_____   _____

_____   _____

_____   _____

Now go back and cross out all your potential weaknesses, because we all have them, and I have learned that when we focus on our strengths, they provide all the ammunition for shooting for the stars that we will ever need. I recently attended a conference and heard the well-known and brilliant speaker, Marcus Buckingham, who is the prodigy at Gallup who created Strengthsfinder. He shared a new perspective on strengths and weaknesses that I really appreciate. He reminded us that we were taught about our weaknesses as our "areas for improvement;" meaning where we should spend our time getting better, so that we would be more successful, but he then presented a better idea. "What if," he suggested to 10,000 of us, "we looked at our strengths as our areas for improvement!" How much better would we be if we got even better at those things we are already good at? Doesn't that make more sense? It sure did to me, and I bet it does to you too. Focus on your strengths, and you will realize your full potential.

Now, looking back at what you do well, what you love to do, and what you are ideally suited to do, given your skills and passion, you may be in the right job now, or if you are looking, then maybe you know what specific type of job will be the best one for you. If not, you may need to change jobs or redefine what it is about the job you have that can capture the passion and the desire that you had as a child. If "fireman" was your heartfelt answer in the third grade, and you are an accountant today, than perhaps the thrill of solving an accounting crisis is where you can sense a bit of the passion that you once felt. If there is no place that your passion is inspired by your current occupation, then you already know it is time to reset your sights, and focus your goals toward a new career, but either way, it is time to clearly define your goals, and to define success in your terms.

Write down your perfect job in detail on the next page. It may be the perfect job you defined earlier, but look at that description again, and refine it here according to your strengths.

My Greatest Passion

Try not to say simply "travel" or "start a foundation" because that is what everyone says at first. Think about what you are passionate about that is also something you could actually see yourself doing for the rest of your life. Use the space below to answer this question: what is your greatest passion...

_____

_____

_____

_____

Defining Success

"If you don't design your own life plan, changes are you'll fall into someone's else's plan. Any guess what they have planned for you? Not much." Jim Rohn

You have discovered your passion, now what? It is time to take an inventory of where you are, compared to where you want to be. This inventory must include all the areas of your life, because success is not one-dimensional. Success is defined by having all areas of your life working in harmony, and toward a worthy goal.

Before you set goals, let's see where you are starting from right now. I suggest looking at the following areas of your life, and writing down EXACTLY where you are at this point, making note of what is working, and what is not:

Here is where I am at right now:

- Physical

  _____

  _____

  _____

- Spiritual

  _____

  _____

  _____

- Family

  _____

  _____

  _____

- Friends

_____

_____

_____

- Financial/Work

_____

_____

_____

These are not listed in any particular order, but together they define what and who you are right now, and provide a means by which you can see where you are in your journey for complete success, and more importantly, they help to start you thinking about who you will become.

I have always defined success not as a reflection of where you are today, but rather, by how far you have come, measured from wherever you started. There is another famous definition of success, that has been attributed to Ralph Waldo Emerson:

"To laugh often and much; To win the respect of intelligent people and the affection of children; To earn the appreciation of honest critics and endure the betrayal of false friends; To appreciate beauty, to find the best in others; To leave the world a bit better, whether by a healthy child, a garden patch or a redeemed social condition; To know even one life has breathed easier because you have lived. This is to have succeeded."

Success truly can be defined in many ways. Here are a few notable quotes on success that have been attributed to some people you might recognize:

> *"Of course there is no formula for success except perhaps an unconditional acceptance of life and what it brings."*
>
> —Arthur Rubinstein

> *"You always pass failure on the way to success."*
>
> —Mickey Rooney

"A successful individual typically sets his next goal somewhat but not too much above his last achievement. In this way he steadily raises his level of aspiration."

—Kurt Lewin

"To follow, without halt, one aim: There's the secret of success."

—Anna Pavlova

"Eighty percent of success is showing up."

—Woody Allen

"I owe my success to having listened respectfully to the very best advice, and then going away and doing the exact opposite."

—G. K. Chesterton

How do you define success? That is truly the only measure of success that matters. Think back to your passion, and define success in the only terms that matter...yours. Realize that you cannot arrive at a destination without first knowing where that destination is relative to where you are starting your journey. To this end, take an honest inventory of where you are today and define a destination, then, set your goals, wisely. Too many of us have spent a lifetime climbing the ladder of success, only to realize that it was leaning against the wrong wall. What does success mean to you, and only you?

Write down your own definition of success:

_____

_____

_____

_____

_____

Now let's spend some time reflecting on your definition of success, in light of your passion, and more specifically, considering where you see yourself today, right now. Look back at what you wanted to be when you grew up. Look again at your strengths and weaknesses, and what activities fill you with passion and joy. Ask friends and family what career by which they could see you ideally successful, and more importantly, why? Take a good mental inventory, and even an actual written inventory of what all these attributes say about who you are. Really think about these questions, and write down your thoughts here: (If you are not sure what you are thinking, then just start writing *anything*, and keep writing until the next page is completely full!)

_____

_____

_____

_____

_____

_____

_____

_____

_____

_____

_____

_____

_____

_____

_____

_____

_____

_____

Now we are going to discover a new way to see yourself, your strengths and weaknesses, and better understand who you are. We are going to learn about your unique *Personality Style.*

Your Personality Style

Man's main task in life is to give birth to himself, to become what he potentially is. The most important product of his effort is his own personality." Erich Fromm

You may not even be familiar with the term *Personality Style*, but its origins go back thousands of years. In fact, some of the earliest recorded personality styles and personality typing compared human personalities to the 4 (four) elements known at that time; earth, fire, water and air. Is easy to see where someone who would be defined as a person with a *fire* personality style, might be considered hot tempered, or driven to succeed. A person defined by the element, *water*, was considered more flexible and easygoing.

You can begin to see how people can be grouped by their individual personality styles. As far back as we know there have generally been four quadrants into which all people have been placed, or categorized. Hippocrates (430-270 Bc) developed the four humours: choleric, melancholic, sanguine, and phlegmatic.

More modern versions of personality styles or personality evaluation testing, such as Myers Briggs, DiSC (the personality methodology defined by William Marston in the 40's, often defined as Driver, Influencer, Steadiness and Conscientious types), or Insights Discovery, divide these four types even further into as many as 16 different categories, or even 72 different personality styles. The bottom line is to understand that there are many ways to determine your unique personality style, and going through exercises to learn your own personality style is one of the most important steps you can take to better understand who you are and what makes you tick.

Most of the training that I have done over the years revolves around personality styles, and each time we introduce these principles to new audiences they are amazed at how accurate the results are, and how eager they are to put this new knowledge into practice. You may already be familiar with some terms used to describe personality traits, such as extrovert, introvert, dominant, etc. You may also be familiar with myriad companies and tests that are used to determine people's personality types and styles, such as the afore mentioned programs like Insights Discovery, Inscape Publishing, DISC, The Platinum Rule, Herman Brain, Profiles International, and Myers Briggs. These sample companies and tests all provide a basic framework by which one can determine one's unique personality type, and some can even generate a 20-30 page report, describing an individual's type, and that person's strengths and weaknesses, based upon the test results. Short of taking one of the tests, our intention here is to give you a basic description of the classic four types, and also help you put yourself into one of the four buckets, to get an introduction into your own personality style, and what it means to you as we continue further into this material.

The basic understanding you will gain here is by no means complete, but it will be enough information for you to both assess more clearly what your type says about you, and also, it will provide a framework into which you can put people you meet, clients, your boss, spouse, and family members so that you can better understand where they are all coming from, and what makes them tick as well.

To introduce you to a four personality type model, we will use the following labels to describe four basic personality types: **Thinker, Director, Relater and Talker.**

Now we will arrange the four types into a graph, with four quadrants. As you can start to guess.

As you can start to guess, you will be predominately one of these four types. Some of you will have a primary type, and possibly a secondary type. Some labels have been added into this graph we have developed to further illustrate where you best fit. We will do this, by first adding four more descriptors at the top, bottom, and right and left sides of the graph. The first two descriptors represent a scale from the left to the right, as shown:

What the words "Introvert" and "Extrovert" represent are really your preferences, meaning that in general, you either tend to tell others what to do, you are outgoing, and get your energy from being around other people, which is extroversion; or, you prefer to ask what needs to be done, you get your energy from being alone, and that you like to keep to yourself, which is introversion. Either trait has its merits, and no one trait by itself is any better or any worse, but we all exhibit a preference. On the graph above, make a mark on the line between introversion and extroversion that best represents where you see yourself as being most comfortable.

As you can see, you have now selected either the right side, or the left side of the graph. In doing so, have excluded two of the four choices as your dominant personality type.

Now let's add another scale on the vertical axis, task versus relationship, shown here:

Again, you must choose where to place yourself on this new scale. You either prefer making decisions based upon tasks that need to be completed, and getting things done and accomplished, or you prefer making decisions dealing with people, with their emotions, and with relationships. Make a mark on the vertical line above on the axis which best describes where you are most comfortable.

Now draw 2 lines to connect the two marks that you have made, and where they meet is likely the personality quadrant that describes you best.

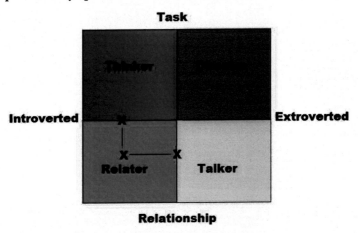

What you have just done, in its most basic form, is placed yourself into only one of the four quadrants. You are now a Director, Relater, Thinker or a Talker. To confirm that this exercise has placed you correctly into the right quadrant, look at the following descriptions of each personality type, and see if in fact it describes you accurately.

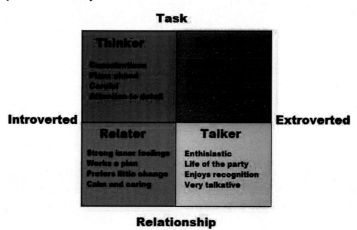

Now, which type are you?

Did you realize that you behave this way? Many people spend their entire lives exhibiting traits like these listed above, without ever realizing that this is the way they are wired, and that they have both strengths, and weaknesses, as a result of which personality type they identify with most. As an example, think of a CEO of a company, who is a Director, which might be a good fit, or how about someone who teaches, a job that a Relater might enjoy very much. Imagine a stand-up comedian; he/she might be a Talker, and an accountant just might be a Thinker.

You can begin to see how your personality type is an excellent data point to consider as you focus in on what work is important to you, and also what you might enjoy doing most. And remember, any personality type can do any job, however, knowing your own unique style will help you better understand why you like certain roles, and not others. Be open to self-discovery, as all growth, personally and professionally, starts with you.

I have taken dozens of personality assessments over the years, and the results are always the same. I am primarily a Talker, and secondly a Director. My wife, Linda is primarily a Director, and secondly a Talker. When we both behave like Directors, we butt heads, as you might imagine, but when we both are behaving like Talkers, we really have a lot of fun together.

Getting to know yourself better is truly a benefit of personality types, and understanding other people's types, based upon their preferences which you observe, is also a benefit. Being able to read other people, and recognize what type they prefer enables you to adapt your style, at times, to better relate to them. An example would be when you, a Talker, are dealing with someone who is doing your taxes, and is likely a Thinker. You would know to hold back some of your exuberance, and stick more to the facts, which in turn, will make your accountant more comfortable dealing with you.

What type is your spouse, partner of significant other?

_____

Name a Thinker, or a Relater that you know:

_____

The greatest salespeople and managers have learned to read people all the time, and adapt their particular style at times, to create rapport with people they deal with, and to get more accomplished in less time. Not surprisingly, most of the training I do now centers around teaching people how to understand the four quadrants, and how people can learn who they are, and then accentuate their positives, and minimize their potential weaknesses. Remember what type you are as we move forward in setting goals that are right for you, and take advantage of your particular style. If your personality style was not so easy to determine using this chapter, consider taking an online assessment. The top three I would recommend are:

Insights Discovery	www.discoveryourself.com
Myers-Briggs	www.cpp.com
DiSC	www.inscapepublishing.com

Please consider taking one of the many personality assessments available, to help you better understand your personality style. Knowing more about how you are wired will help you in your job search and in every other area of your life as well.

Additional resources are listed at the back of this book, if you are interested in learning even more about personality styles. Now it's time to set your goals.

Setting Goals

"Setting goals is the first step in turning the invisible into the visible."

—*Tony Robbins*

Now it is time to set your goals, select your destination, chart your course, for a definite, and successful future. If you haven't set goals for yourself before, there is an excellent acronym that can help you. The acronym is SMART, and leads you to setting SMART goals.

SMART goals are:

Simple

Measurable

Attainable

Results Oriented

Time Sensitive

Spend time reflecting on your goals, in light of your passion, and where you are at today. Think about your particular personality style, and what you want to accomplish, given who you are, and what you do best.

My Goals

- Physical

_____

_____

_____

- Spiritual

  _____

  _____

  _____

- Family

  _____

  _____

  _____

- Friends

  _____

  _____

  _____

- Financial/Work

  _____

  _____

  _____

For the last 21 years, since a friend first shared the "secret" of goal-setting with me at age 25, I have written down my goals every year, and posted them on my bathroom mirror, where I see them, and re-read them every morning and every evening. If you take only one action after reading this guidebook, please, please, please WRITE DOWN YOUR GOALS and READ THEM EVERYDAY! You too, will succeed, and live your life happy every day for the life you lead, and the joy that you bring to others as a result.

As further proof this formula works, here are a few of my goals that I wrote down, and have read every day for the last ten years. As I write this guidebook, these were all written down, and have all come true:

> Be a business leader
> Take a year off
> Fly fish in Colorado
> Take an ocean vacation
> Write a book
> Fly in a helicopter

Golf in Scotland

Win a golf tournament

As I achieve some of the goals that I have set for myself, I replace them with others:

Fly in a fighter jet

Speak fluent Spanish

Learn sign language

Climb Kilimanjaro

Speak to 10,000 people

Get SCUBA Certified

Visit Tibet

An excellent way for you to post your goals, and track your success every day is to buy a dry erase marker pen, the kind that are used to write on whiteboards. This is what I use to write my goals down on my bathroom mirror even today, and it is what you can use, too. You can purchase the markers from any office supply store, and I strongly suggest that you do. If you are truly committed to success, then get the markers, and write down your goals on the mirror that you look into each morning, and again each night. This is so simple, but I promise you, less than 10% of the people that purchased this guidebook will do even this much, but the wealth accumulated by those 10% will be greater than the other 90% combined. Be a success; be in that 10%. Do it. Do it right now.

Learning to Think!

"Creative thinking inspires ideas. Ideas inspire change."

—*Barbara Januszklewicz*

There is a famous recording made by Earl Nightingale in 1956, called "The Strangest Secret". A friend gave it to me when I was 22-years-old, and it changed my life. In fact, I have heard that it is the first recording featuring the spoken word to ever become a million seller. It is not as famous today as it once was, but its message is timeless. Mr. Nightingale suggests that even though we all desired at one time to be successful, we simply forgot about it over time. Incredible! We could never forget our goals, our passion, our mission for success, could we? That sad truth is that we can, and most of us have. Still trying to remember what your passion was, and is today? If you haven't thought about it recently, then you have forgotten, and that is the single most important factor in your success, or lack of success, in everything you do.

To begin to really understand this powerful concept, we need to go back to the beginning. For me, this means going back to the Bible, where we have all read or heard the phrase, " ... for whatever a man sows, that he will also reap," Galations 6:7. Growing up in a small town in Wisconsin I took this as a child and through my teen years to mean that if someone cleared their fields, planted good seeds, and tended their crops diligently, they would enjoy a bountiful harvest in the fall. What I didn't realize until I was 23-years-old was that it means so much more; that this simple phrase holds the key to all the success that I have had in my life, and that it holds the key for your success as well.

Having spent 25 years in the computer training business, it is impossible for me not to cite a metaphor that those of you with a personal computer, or access to one, will immediately understand. For the rest of you, just stay with me, and I'll bring it all back around. At the heart of every computer is a processor, Intel being probably the most famous. This processor can do no more, and no less than execute the commands that it has received. If the input is good data, or good information, then the processor executes the commands, and returns good data, good information. Simple really, and the same data running through the same computer will return the same results time after time, after time.

Technology folks have summarized this concept in an acronym, "GIGO" which stands for "garbage in, garbage out". Input good data, get good results, input bad data … you get the idea, "GIGO". Remember this, because this is where the metaphor hits home, and unfortunately, this is what most of us are doing unconsciously with our minds all the time, the most powerful computer the world will ever see.

The Power of our Minds

How many of us really think about the power of our minds? Do you ever wonder how much of our mind's power we really use? According to some experts, the average person consciously uses less than 10% of the computing power of our minds. I suggest that the crime here is not the amount of our minds that we consciously use, but rather the manner by which we use this, our most valuable human asset. What manner is this? It is that we use or program our minds, most of the time unconsciously! We don't even think about the data, or the information that we are putting into our minds in the first place!

As Earle Nightingale said in his famous recording from 1956, "The reason men [and women] are not successful is because they don't *think!* Sure we all go through the motions everyday, in all our actions and all our routines, but how often do we consciously *think*? How often do we *consciously* select good input to put into our minds, so that after our minds process the information, we get good and *predetermined* results; the results that we are really after in the first place, like having a happy marriage, being a good father, or having a successful and rewarding career.

How often do you select the proper input to achieve the desired results that you seek? Not sure how to do this? Intrigued? Read on.

Programming your Mind

Just like in the computer metaphor, our minds are idle, until we give them input to process. We provide this input with what we see, what we hear, what we feel, touch and even taste. Our senses are the only external ways we can define the input, and they shape our thoughts and determine our future. Did you realize there is a much more important means by which we deliver input into our minds? It is through the questions that we ask of ourselves, consciously, subconsciously and even unconsciously.

These inputs are the real and very, very powerful programs that we unleash to run in our minds, and they are running every second of every minute of every day. When the questions are conscious, we often times are not even aware that we are setting these negative programs into motion. It happens when we say to ourselves, "How come I never get a break" or "How come I am so unlucky?" These types of questions, once asked of ourselves, set the world's most powerful computer into motion, trying to resolve the questions, the programs, that we have selected to run, and the power, and the horror, is that once set into motion, these programs use every possible input that they can find to answer the questions we have asked.

Here are a few examples: If we ask ourselves, "How come I never get a break?" Then our minds will seek out and validate every input that satisfies the question.

Our minds will offer up answers, or output like, "The reason I never get a break is that life is unfair, and I will always end up with the short end of the stick."

We may also ask, "Why am I in a dead end job?"

Immediately, our minds will find examples to support our questions, and answer, "You are in a dead end job because you couldn't get a better job even if you tried."

Get it? Are you starting to see how we can influence, and be influenced by what we think about. The message I am sharing with you is that we truly do become what we think about. What do you think about?

What questions do you ask yourself every day? Are they thoughtful, careful questions, like, " How can I do more at work to get a raise?" and " What can I do today to be a better father?" or, are they thoughts like, " Why am I in such a dead end job?" and "Why are people always such a pain?"

Ask, and you shall receive. What are you asking for? Do you know?

Visual, Auditory and Kinesthetic Learners

As I mentioned earlier, input into our minds is received through our five physical senses, and also through a more difficult to understand, "sixth sense" often referred to as intuition. Of these, taste and smell are not statistically significant for us to discuss here, and intuition is very difficult to quantify. Some people believe that intuition represents "the universe" or "energy" or spirituality, while others argue that there is no such thing. If one of these works for you, then use it, if it doesn't, then intuition may not be a tool that you can, or want to rely upon. It begs far more time for discussion than we have here, but keep it in the back of your mind. We are primarily concerned here with the three main senses we use most of the time to receive input into our minds, and which will be defined more clearly here; namely, our sense of sight, (visual) hearing, (auditory) and touch, (kinesthetic).

Our sight, or visual input dominates most of what we all bring into our minds every day. It has been shown that our minds can process visual information that it receives ten times faster than when we hear it, but that our retention tends to be higher when we receive input through our ears. Additionally, some people favor their kinesthetic sense, or their sense of touch. Regardless of which of these three senses you favor most, it is important to be aware that we are in control of what we take in through these senses. If we are primarily visual, then what we CHOOSE to look at determines what we see. If we are primarily auditory, then what we CHOOSE to listen to determines what we hear. If we are primarily kinesthetic, then what we CHOOSE to do determines what we experience.

What input are you CHOOSING each day? Is it a conscious decision? It should be, and especially when you look at, (or hear, or experience) your goals, then you are putting the right thoughts in motion, which will inevitably lead to the predetermined results you seek.

Once you accept and believe that your mind operates in this manner, you will always set the right programs into motion to get what you want. This is the key to success. We all do become what we think about. The problem is not that we are all choosing to program failure and unhappiness into our minds, and into our lives, but rather that we are not consciously programming success into our minds and into our lives.

Sadly, most of us are all operating on autopilot, and the inputs that we are programming into our minds, from the traffic jam on the way to work, to the depressing morning news we watched, to the grumbling and destructive questions we are asking ourselves after skipping breakfast and rushing out the door, late for work almost without realizing that we are doing so, are the wrong programs that then run *all day* in our minds until we CHOOSE to input new programs, and ask ourselves new questions. If you haven't thought about what questions you are asking yourself, and about what inputs you are receiving from other people, television, radio, etc. then you are going nowhere at best, and at worst, you are quietly on a negative path of destruction, blaming others for results that you simply forgot to control, and to determine in advance, based upon your passion, and the goals that you have set for yourself. A sad truth that I have heard in the past is that most of us spend more time planning a weekend vacation, than we do planning for the rest of our lives, and our careers. Is this true for you?

How exciting that we can change this at any time, by following through with the five steps described here so far, and, assuming you have defined goals as a result of what you have read and learned so far, you are on your way to the front of the pack, the top of the mountain of success, where, if I may paraphrase what Earle Nightingale said in his audio book, *Lead the Field*, "When you are on top, the sun rises earlier, sets later, the people are nicer, they smile a lot more, … its nicer up here."

Let's look at how fundamental this programming principle is to all of us. What were your waking thoughts this morning? Were they in alignment with your goals; were they negative, or just neutral? You probably can't even remember, and therefore your subconscious mind, the infinitely powerful part of your mind, that could have been seeking out opportunities throughout the day, to aid you in the completion of your goals, ran on autopilot, *and in the wrong direction!* Let's fix that starting tomorrow, and for the rest of your successful life.

Tonight, write yourself a positive note, an affirmation, such as, "Today I will see the best in other people, whether they cut me off on my drive into work, (maybe they are having a personal crisis, and they need to get into work or they will lose their job, etc.,) or whether they are my coworkers, whom I will compliment whenever I can."

Write down your own affirmation tonight, and set it on your alarm clock, or using a dry erase pen, write it on your bathroom mirror. If you have already written your goals as suggested earlier, then use them. Now, as you awake tomorrow, read the goal list before you are even fully awake, and you will have taken the first true step towards controlling your thoughts, and therefore controlling your future.

If you want to really leverage your sensory inputs, and you should, then read your goals aloud, and feel the excitement that reading them generates. This will enable you to engage all your primary senses to help you realize your goals. DO NOT wake up, turn on the television, or the radio, and listen to all the naysayers describe all the crime, moral decay and financial hardships you will surely face throughout the day. Instead, control the input you receive, and the outcomes you seek will surely follow, as surely as any computer will output the same results, given the same input. Realize too, that your mind, through your five senses, seeks and receives input all day, starting with your waking thoughts, and will return output, in the form of your thoughts and actions, regardless of what you do, so take control now!

There clearly is a set formula for success, that has been at work in our lives since we were born, if we just pay attention. You have learned the first five steps of that process so far, and now there only three more to go!

The first five steps you have learned so far are:

Find your passion

Define success

Know your personality style

Set your goals

Learn to Think!

The final three steps, which are no less important than the first five are:

Operate with Integrity

Execute Daily

Giving Back

These five principles are the first half of the formula for success, used by nearly every happy and successful person I have ever met, and it is the surest way for you to become your best, reach your potential, and live a successful life. At this point I really hope you have written your responses in this book. If you did not, your life will not change, and you have actually chosen *not* to be in that top 10%. If however, you *have* written down your answers honestly to these questions, you are in the top 10%. You are a superstar. You will succeed.

Now let's tackle the last three steps of the *Discover Yourself* formula.

Operate With Integrity

"Integrity is doing the right thing, even when no one is watching."

—*S. Lewis*

In the early 1900s, a lot was written about success. The industrial age enabled men like Andrew Carnegie and Henry Ford to rise as business leaders, and their lives, and their extraordinary success became the subject of many writings and studies. One theme that runs throughout these writings is the character of these successful men, and others from that era. Integrity emerged as one trait that all these men shared, and integrity was credited as a key factor in their success, time and time again. Sadly, in the years from then until now, integrity and character have slid into the shadows, and yet, all the truly successful people that I know own these important traits. I know people, too, who are financially successful, but they are not men and women of character, and their lives are disconnected. Success must be the definition of a whole person, whose goals, actions, thoughts and character are in place, complete, and worthy of exemplification. A person can only lead a life of integrity if both their personal life, and their business life, reflect the same integrity.

We are daily made aware of scandals involving sports figures and celebrities, along with news of questionable financial dealings on Wall Street. Political heroes are placed on a pedestal even while cheating on their wives or their taxes. The media has created the illusion that success can be achieved in the absence of integrity. It cannot. The quality of your character will determine your degree of professional and personal success. The two cannot be separated.

I will never forget, as a child of about 10-years-old, cleaning my father's law office on the weekends to earn a few extra bucks. He came in one weekend while I was working, and made a few phone calls. I saw him make the calls, then write down notes, and put a number beside each note, like .25 hours, or .50 hours. I asked him what the numbers meant, and he shared that it was how he billed his clients, that .25 hours was the charge for a quarter hour, and .50 hours for a half hour of his time. I remember asking him, "Why don't you just write down a bigger number, and charge them more for your work?" He told me that people did business with him because of his integrity, and that if he let it slip, even a little bit, that he would never be able to gain it back. That message has stuck with me all this time. It is often much harder to do the right thing, but the rewards are long-term, and this is what I mean by integrity. We have all heard the phrase, "What goes around, comes around", and nowhere does this ring true as much as it pertains to character. Decide now to make your character exceptional, and the success, and self-confidence that you seek will be yours.

While integrity defines how we conduct ourselves, it can also be used to determine our personal and professional environment. I heard Lance Secretan speak ten years ago at the annual conference for Computer Training Companies. He had written a successful book titled, *Reclaiming Higher Ground*, that I highly recommend. In his speech he shared a few examples of integrity displayed by corporations. One example was the 2% milk that many of us purchase and consume every day. He asked a room of about 400 people what the percentage of fat there was in whole milk. Most of the room raised their hands for 100%. Lance then shared with us that whole milk is only about 4%, and that 2% milk is a misleading indicator of the difference between the two products. It is legal, but is it moral?

A second example that hit home with me was about a jar of spaghetti sauce, labeled "fresh tasting" rather than fresh, because it was really not fresh, but that corporation somehow had its corporate lawyers fight for the right to use the phrase, "fresh tasting". Legal, yes, but moral? How about cigarette companies? Ouch!

Are you looking to work for a company for which you are proud? Make sure integrity defines not just what you do, but where you do it, and with whom.

I recently attended a leadership training session taught by Bill George, the former CEO of Medtronic, sponsored by Tergar Meditation Center, and the University of Minnesota Center for Spirituality and Healing. Spending two days with him was inspiring to me, because he put such great emphasis on integrity, and doing the right thing when it matters most: when we are alone. Such a refreshing message, and one which his books, *Authentic Leadership*, and *True North*, define and clarify so well. Make integrity a cornerstone of your life, and spend your life with others who do the same.

Basic Flowchart

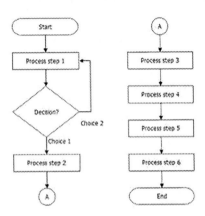

Execution

"Action (execution) is the foundational key to all success." Anonymous

No guidebook to a having a successful life and the perfect job could ever be complete without a commentary on execution. That is, the mean by which we accomplish all that we set out to do. Defining goals based upon your passion, thinking about them, and operating with integrity will not lead to any sustainable amount of success, unless you are committed to staying the course, and EXECUTING your plans for the attainment of your goals. For some people, success and financial rewards have come too soon, and without the monotonous daily rigors of execution. Easily won riches will be easily lost, but hard earned wages are your ticket to lasting success.

Let's take some time and define the plans you will use to secure the attainment of the goals that you have defined earlier in this guidebook.

What are the key components of the plan that you will need to execute, in order to achieve the goals that you have defined for yourself? Write down now what you will need to do, and how often, to achieve the goals that you have set for yourself:

How I Will EXECUTE to Achieve My Goals

- Physical

  _____

  _____

  _____

- Spiritual

  _____

  _____

  _____

- Family

  _____

  _____

  _____

- Friends

  _____

  _____

  _____

- Financial/Work

_____

_____

_____

Now let's expand this last section, Financial/Work, in greater detail. Here are a few more questions that will make the difference in finding the ideal career, one which fits you, your skills, and your passion.

What job, at which company, and in what industry?

How will you research your choices?

How will you market yourself?

How will you network with others?

Who will support you?

What job boards, newspapers, and web sites will you read regularly?

What career seminars will you attend?

What motivational tapes and CDs will you listen to?

What additional books will you read?

How many new contacts will you make each day?

Are you on LinkedIn.com?

Are you on Facebook.com?

Does Craigslist.com have your perfect job listed?

What trade associations could you join?

Can you call the company president directly?

How many contacts can you find through your friends?

Are there state and/or federal jobs available?

What government programs can you access?

Can your church help you succeed?

Are you committed to doing what it takes to succeed?

I could add five or fifty-five more blank pages here, but it is easier to send you to your laptop where you can start to do the homework necessary to really know what is right for you, and where your best gifts will best shine. It is really up to you to define your plans, at whatever level of detail it takes for you to succeed. If creating the plan necessary to achieve your goals is difficult, or you need help, email me your goals at *scott@ discoveryourself.com*, and I'll offer any assistance I can to help you define what you need to do to succeed. Do not continue reading until you have answered at least a few of the previous questions. Your future depends on it!

Believe it or not, defining one's plan is not the area where most of us fail, but rather in not defining WHAT we are setting out to do, or not having the motivation to pursue the goals that we have set for ourselves. *Where there is a will, there is a way.* Have you ever heard this phrase before? Do not lose heart if defining your plan is more difficult that you thought it would be. Keep looking back at your goals, stay in touch with your passion, and realize that you will find a way. Thomas Edison, upon documenting that his 10,000 attempts at identifying the right filament for his soon to be perfected incandescent bulb, did not work, was reportedly asked how it felt to fail 10,000 times. To which Mr. Edison reportedly answered, "I have not failed, I have successfully eliminated 10,000 filaments which do not work!" Such a restated, positive

Scott Schwefel

attitude about failure maybe the one necessary element that leads so many to their eventual success; a badge of honor that all the successful entrepreneurs that I know wear with pride.

Another aspect of your plan, and the execution of it, is to realize that even before the ink is dry, (even as it rolls off your printer), that it will be obsolete almost immediately. People change, circumstances change, but what rarely changes is our passions, and if we have defined our goals thoughtfully and in light of our passions, then they will remain consistent also. They serve as the lighthouse that will direct us steadfastly toward goals that we are passionate about. The purpose of a plan of execution is to serve as a roadmap which we understand will change over time. It serves as a guidepost to show us how we are doing in our quest towards our goals. Stay the course and you will succeed.

The hardest aspect of the execution of your plan (remembering that execution itself is not the hardest part of your success formula, but that rather defining

100

what you want and why, is really where most people fail) is to do what needs to be done, when it needs to be done, in order to see the completion of your goals. A great question I often ask myself as I look on my own plans, especially at times of weakness, is "If I look back an hour from now, what actions should I take that will leave me the most satisfied *after the action has been completed?*" I don't mean to pretend that I always take the right actions afterwards, but I *always* know which action I *should* have chosen.

Another way is to ask yourself, "What would the person that I plan to become do right now?" Print both these questions on a postcard, and carry them with you, because even as you are focused on execution, what matters most is to *think*! Think about why you are choosing to execute your plan, what is it about the plan that drives you toward your passion, and how good it feels to succeed? Look to the lighthouse that is your goals, to help you through the tough times.

Weight loss is a great example of where these questions or another phrase that I have heard fits into our day-to-day, decision-making process. The phrase is, "Nothing tastes as good as being thin feels." (Try it when you're hungry.) Successful execution of our plans to make our goals is an everyday, all the time thing. We will all fail at times to stay the course, but success is achieved when we get back up after we have fallen; when we climb back on the horse that threw us; when we jump back on the bicycle and keep riding. A Chinese proverb simply states, "Fall down seven times, get up eight".

What enables us to do this is the endgame. It is our lighthouse; our GOALS, fueled with the all the passion that we have been able to muster as we defined them, read them every morning and again every evening, and consumed them through our senses every day.

Thinking daily about your goals is the surest way to sustain yourself, especially when executing the plan becomes difficult. No one achieves lasting success without getting through the tough spots. If you have defined the right goals which you are passionate about, then you have all the ammunition you will ever need to keep you going, through all the difficulties that you encounter. Remember, anything worth getting is worth fighting for. Are you willing to fight to achieve your goals? If so, then you will succeed.

Giving Back

"Since you get more joy out of giving joy to others, you should put a good deal of thought into the happiness you are able to give."

—*Eleanor Roosevelt*

Let's jump ahead in your life one year. You have made significant progress towards your stated goals. In fact, you have even achieved a few of them, and also added a few more. You have a new job that you love, and whose mission and values matches your own. You are physically fit, and proud of the person whom you have become. You wake up passionately every day, re-read your goals, and enter your day pursuing those worthy goals through your intentional and passionate thoughts and actions. You have plans for execution in place that help steer you in the right direction, you are on top, secure in the knowledge that you have unlocked the secret to success, and carry yourself with more self-confidence than you ever thought possible.

Now what?

Now is just the beginning. Now is when it starts to get really fun, because now you have put yourself in a position to give back. Give back your time, your talents, your joy, your money, yourself. It is time to give back that part of you that makes a difference in the lives of others.

One of the ways that I have always enjoyed giving back is to share books. As I have read books throughout my life, I have given away thousands of them to people that I knew would benefit. In fact, I founded the web site www.selfconfidence.com in 1996 simply because I couldn't keep up, as I was buying certain books, one or two at a time, to give to other people whom I would meet often while traveling. So I set up the site to allow people to jump online and learn key concepts about success and also order the books themselves. I get great joy out of hearing back from someone that a book or tape that I gave them helped them achieve their goals, and I have realized, as many of us do, as we grow older, that there is much greater satisfaction in helping others, than there is in helping ourselves. The catch is, to really be able to help other people; we need to have at least operated our own lives in a way that sustains our ability to give back, whether that means giving our time, our talents or our other resources. Hopefully, your new understanding of the principles of success will put you well on your way to being able to give back, more than you ever thought you could.

What will you give back to the world? When? Giving should be a key part of your personal plan for success. As you work through this document, you may be struggling financially, or searching for deeper meaning in your life, but you still are able to begin giving back right now. It may mean offering a smile to the checkout clerk, allowing the obnoxious driver, intent on cutting you off, merge in front of you, or even providing more warmth for your spouse and your family through kinder words and deeds.

Opportunities to give back exists every day, and the more we take advantage of them, the more it is affirmed that we really do control our own destiny, and that although we cannot control the circumstances around us, what we *can* always control is our response to those circumstances, and our surroundings.

We are all responsible, meaning, that we are all

response able,

We are able to **choose our response**, at any time, to whatever happens to us.

Never again say "I have to…" or " I need to…" instead teach yourself to say "I choose to…" in every circumstance, because it is *true!* Everything that happens in our lives that we do, we choose to do. This single most fundamental concept will change the way you look at every aspect of your life. Start saying "I choose to…" today. Reinforce the concept that you really are in charge of your destiny.

When I grew up, my parents had a plaque on the wall in our hallway, which I read every day, but the significance of the words on the plague did not hit me until I was about 30-years-old. Its author is anonymous, and I have heard it described as "The Serenity Prayer".

God, grant me the serenity
To accept the things
That I cannot change,

The courage to change

The things that I can, and

The wisdom

To know

The difference.

I never gave much thought to this prayer as I grew up, but, it was burned into my subconscious because I saw it every day. Later in life, I discovered its meaning and now I think of its words all the time. Its real meaning to me is:

God, grant me the serenity
To accept

WHAT HAPPENS TO ME!

The courage to change
HOW I RESPOND! And

The wisdom
To know
The difference.

I suggest that you find a phrase, poem or prayer that reminds you that we are all in charge of our destiny; that we are always able to choose how we respond in any given situation, and that those of us who count ourselves among people who are successful, are living a life on purpose, moving in the direction of worthy goals, and able to give back to others at any time, for the sole purpose of helping others and helping to make the world a better place. Post your favorite motivating poem, saying, prayer on your mirror, put a copy in your car, and at your office, and even on your refrigerator.

Earl Nightingale said 50 years ago, *"We become what we think about."*

It is written in the Bible, *"As a man thinketh in his heart, so is he,"* *Proverbs 23:7.*

Even Buddha said, *"What we think, we become."*

What are you waiting for?

Steps **1 2 3 4 5 6 7 8**

Conclusion

There is a formula for success, and it has now been shared with you in eight steps. You now know that you are responsible for your own personal degree of happiness, success and self-confidence, and you can no longer blame others. Each day, when you look in the mirror, be sure to smile at the person that can make all your dreams come true, and when necessary, review the 8 steps summarized again for you here:

Step 1. Find Your Passion—What would you do if you had all the money, and all the time in the world? What parts of your job and your life are consistent with your passion?

Step 2. Define Success—In the only terms that matter, yours.

Step 3. Know your Personality Style–Use this knowledge to achieve your goals, and take an assessment to learn more.

Scott Schwefel

Step 4. Set Goals—Set SMART goals around every area of your life, and write them down. Read them every morning, and again at night.

> Physical
>
> Spiritual
>
> Family
>
> Friends
>
> Financial/Work

Step 5. Think!–Post your goals, and read them daily, to define your thoughts, which will shape your daily actions, which will lead you inevitably to your successful future. Use the unlimited power of your mind.

Step 6. Operate with Integrity—Your personal life cannot be separated from your professional life, so in both aspects, live your life in such a way that it exemplifies a man or woman of character. Be a person of great character in all your endeavors, and choose wisely those with whom you spend your time.

112

Step 7. Execute—Clearly write down a plan that helps you move towards your goals. Remember that your passion and goals will sustain you through the hard times, but never give up, never quit.

Step 8. Give back—Success, when measured by what you alone achieve, will never sustain you long term. Start now giving out a smile when you can, a helping hand, and realize you are planting the seeds of giving in your life that will enable you to look back on a long life, and feel it was well lived. God bless you in your journey. I wish you all the success in the world, and if I can aid you in the completion of your goals, then email them to me at scott@discoveryourself.com and let's arrive at your final, successful destination together.

Successfully,

Scott Schwefel

P.S. Remember the promise I made to you at the beginning of this book? If you have faithfully read the entire book, and completed all the written exercises, and are still not where you want to be, please contact me at scott@discoveryourself.com, and when I receive your book, with the completed exercises, I'll refund your purchase price, and your shipping costs. Guaranteed.

About the Author

Scott Schwefel was raised in Beaver Dam, Wisconsin, by parents that taught him the value of finding one's passion, goal setting, hard work, integrity and the need to give back. He attended the University of Minnesota to study engineering, then later received his degree from Concordia University in Organizational Development and Communications. He launched several startup companies in his early twenties, and also sold computers to pay the rent each month. In 1989 he and his partners raised nearly a million dollars in venture capital, and built and sold a multimillion dollar food company. He married his wife, Linda, in 1989, and together they began teaching, writing and defining the principles in this guidebook, by launching a sales training company in 1991.

In 1995 Mr. Schwefel founded Benchmark Learning, which he grew to become Minnesota's largest technology training center. During this time, he interviewed more than 500 job candidates, and realized that there were a small number of people who although in a job search, were totally in control of their destiny, and it showed. He began to understand why *these* job candidates were different from the others, and how they understood the principles in this book. After a transformative month living with the Massai and Hadza tribes in Tanzania, Africa, he returned home, sold his interest in Benchmark for more than a million dollars to take a year off and write this book on the principles of success that helped him personally succeed.

Scott is available for speaking, training and coaching engagements on any of the principles contained in this guidebook. He enjoys delivering keynotes to thousands, conducting small group workshops, or one-on-one mentoring of CEOs and Executives.

You may contact Scott at scott@discoveryourself.com or by phone at 952-454-4065, or by visiting www.scottschwefel.com to learn more.

**Additional recommended reading, or
audio book selections, by the Author:**

The Strangest Secret by Earl Nightingale

The Psychology of Achievement by Brian Tracy

The Psychology of Selling by Brian Tracy

Repacking Your Bags by Richard Leider

Lead the Field by Earl Nightingale

How to Win Friends and Influence People by Dale
Carnegie

Think and Grow Rich by Napolean Hill

Do What You Love, The Money Will Follow by
Marsha Sinetar

The E-Myth by Michael Gerber

Authentic Leadership by Bill George

True North by Bill George

Scott's keynote speaking videos, and more books
available at: www.ScottSchwefel.com

Personality Assessments, and related training seminars and webinars are also available at: www.DiscoverYourself.com

listen|imagine|view|experience

AUDIO BOOK DOWNLOAD INCLUDED WITH THIS BOOK!

In your hands you hold a complete digital entertainment package. In addition to the paper version, you receive a free download of the audio version of this book. Simply use the code listed below when visiting our website. Once downloaded to your computer, you can listen to the book through your computer's speakers, burn it to an audio CD or save the file to your portable music device (such as Apple's popular iPod) and listen on the go!

How to get your free audio book digital download:

1. Visit www.tatepublishing.com and click on the e|LIVE logo on the home page.
2. Enter the following coupon code:
   59ae-e406-105c-d10e-79b2-2ee0-5173-ead7
3. Download the audio book from your e|LIVE digital locker and begin enjoying your new digital entertainment package today!